IGNACY JAN PADEREWSKI

Polish Pianist and Patriot

Champions of Freedom

IGNACY JAN PADEREWSKI

Polish Pianist and Patriot

Elaine Slivinski Lisandrelli

MORGAN REYNOLDS Incorporated

Greensboro

IGNACY JAN PADEREWSKI:
Polish Pianist and Patriot

Library of Congress Cataloging-in-Publication Data
Lisandrelli, Elaine Slivinski.
  Ignacy Jan Paderewski : Polish pianist and patriot / Elaine
Slivinski Lisandrelli
     p. cm
  Includes bibliographical references and indes.
  Summary: A biography of the Polish piano virtuoso who became the first
prime minister of a united Poland after World War I.
  ISBN 1-883846-29-3
  1. Paderewski, Ignacy Jan, 1860-1941. 2. Pianists--Poland-
-Biography. 3. Statesmen--Poland--Biography. [1. Paderewski,
Ignacy Jan, 1860-1941. 2. Pianists. 3. Statesmen. 4. Poland-
-Biography.] I. Title.
ML3930.P17L57   1998
786.2'092--dc21
[B}   98-37784
                                     CIP
                                   MN AC

Dedication

*Dedicated to all the noble hearts
who strive to keep
Paderewski's memory alive.*

Contents

Ignacy Jan Paderewski
(Ig-not-see Yawn Pa-de-rev-skee)

Chapter One

Boyhood Dreams

On a cold night in 1863, over one hundred Russian Cossacks on horseback encircled a house in the village of Kurylowka. Cossacks burst inside the house and searched for papers, uniforms, and guns. They seized a man named Jan Paderewski. His three-year-old son, Ignacy, and five-year old daughter, Antonina, watched in terror as their father was taken from their home. They had no mother to protect them. She had died a few months after Ignacy's birth. "What is happening to my father?" Ignacy asked. One of the Cossacks laughed as he hit the boy several times with his whip. Mr. Paderewski was dragged off to prison because he was suspected of supporting an anti-Russian revolt. Alone, the Paderewski children watched their village burn.

Ignacy Jan Paderewski grew up to be one of Poland's finest composers and one of the world's greatest pianists. In the early 1900s, his concerts were sold out weeks in advance. Millions of people of all ages wanted to meet him and get his autograph. As a concert pianist, he knew the adoration that certain Hollywood stars know today. He eventually sat with presidents and kings, but he never forgot that tragic scene of his childhood. He used his fame as a musician to inform the world of Poland's struggle for freedom, and he used his fortune to help the world.

After that terrifying night in 1863, a kindly aunt took Ignacy and Antonina to live with her. The children missed their father terribly. To ease the loneliness, Ignacy soon learned to read and to write letters to his father in prison.

A year later, Mr. Paderewski was released from prison. By his father's side, Ignacy heard stories of times past. Ignacy learned how his mother, Polixena Nowicki Paderewski, an accomplished musician, had been born in exile in snowy Siberian lands. Her father, a law professor, and her mother also had been jailed because of their opposition to the rulers that had taken Poland's land. Ignacy learned of Poland's long, proud history.

When Ignacy Jan Paderewski was born on November 6, 1860, Poland had disappeared from the European map. Over the years, three powerful countries—Russia, Austria, and Prussia—had divided Poland and ruled each part as their own. Although Ignacy lived in the Russian part, deep in his heart he knew it was still Poland. Although he couldn't point to Poland on the map, he held onto his Polish roots and made it his goal to reunite the divided pieces of his country. In his childhood games, he liked to be a soldier. Dressed in a uniform of red and white paper made by his sister, Ignacy brandished a hand-carved wooden sword and rode a horse made of sticks and bags. In these boyhood battles, he always saved Poland. Even as a young boy, he hoped to become somebody important so he could help Poland.

Holding onto his Polish identity was not easy. Ignacy and other Poles had been forbidden to celebrate their heritage. Publicly, Poles couldn't dress in their native costume or sing patriotic songs. Russian censors had banned patriotic works by Polish poets, novelists, playwrights, painters, and sculptors. But, musicians had discovered a way to

The Paderewski children: Antonina and Ignacy.

express their love for their divided country without being punished. They wove their hatred of tyranny and hope for freedom into the rich fabric of music where it couldn't be detected by censors. Music told Poland's story. Ignacy could come to Poland's rescue as a musician.

Michael Babianski, one of Ignacy's teachers, encouraged his patriotism and his longing to help his country. As was common in Poland in his day, Ignacy's schooling took place at home. His father had hired Babianski to live with the family and tutor his children. Ignacy and Mr. Babianski read historical novels, discussed wars both past and present, and shared their dreams of Poland regaining freedom.

Because Polish newspapers were forbidden, Ignacy learned Russian to keep up with the news. On winter evenings in a candlelit room, Mr. Paderewski and his friends crowded around Ignacy. They couldn't read Russian, and he proudly read aloud to them. Sometimes when there was no good news to report, he changed the bad news into good news as he read.

Some of these inaccurate newspaper readings got Ignacy into trouble. During the Franco-Prussian War, Ignacy and his father's friends rooted for the French who were being destroyed by the Prussians. As Ignacy held the newspaper in front of him, he lied because he didn't have the heart to tell them the truth. "The French are safely at Cologne," he reported. His listeners cheered and celebrated the French "victory" with glasses of fine wine!

Ignacy's false reports continued for several weeks. He enjoyed this game and delighted in making everyone happy, but he sensed that sooner or later the truth would appear. One day, after Mr. Paderewski had returned from a doctor's visit miles away from home, it did.

Mr. Paderewski insisted on seeing the newspapers that his son had read, but Ignacy burned them in the oven.

Ignacy's father accused him of lying and ranted about how foolish he had felt when his doctor told him that the "good news" of the French "victories" wasn't accurate. He reminded Ignacy of the real truth that the French were being defeated at every battle.

"I did not lie," Ignacy's deep-set blue eyes welled with tears. "I only read what I hoped—what you wanted."

Ignacy received "a few hard whacks" from his father, but one of Mr. Paderewski's friends interceded for the boy. Soon, Mr. Paderewski forgave his son. He realized Ignacy only wanted to make his listeners happy.

Mr. Paderewski was strict with his son, but Ignacy felt he treated him fairly and appreciated his belief in him. The boy's attraction to the small, battered piano in the Paderewski home pleased his father. Even at three and four years old, Ignacy pressed one finger on the keys, searched for the melodies and delighted in the sounds he created. In his pre-teenage years, when his father was ill, Ignacy improvised for him hour after hour. As he played, he made up a variety of melodies including minuets and waltzes.

One birthday his father gave him a handmade blank book inscribed *Compositions of Ignacy Jan Paderewski*. The boy filled the book with short musical pieces created by selecting notes that looked attractive on the page rather than notes that would produce an appealing melody. Years later, Ignacy carefully crafted musical compositions by paying more attention to sound than to just pretty notes on a page.

Unfortunately, no skilled music teachers lived nearby. His instructors, although kind individuals, lacked the musical background to give him the technical knowledge he needed. As a ten-year-old, Ignacy had no knowledge of the correct hand position and proper fingering, yet he played beautifully. He loved the freedom of improvising, but he disliked preparing for music lessons and practicing chords and scales. He often hid in treetops to avoid his lessons and practice sessions.

Even though they had no musical library and lived far away from the cities and artistic centers, the Paderewski children played operatic themes given to them by one of their teachers. Ignacy and his sister appeared at some informal neighborhood concerts. While their four hands shared one piano and brought some of the operas of Donizetti and Rossini to life, they playfully jabbed elbows and occasionally kicked each other's feet.

At small concerts, Ignacy played to delighted audiences. Sometimes members of the audience asked him to perform the wet-towel trick. Igancy obliged by covering the keyboard with a wet towel and playing every note correctly! His fame spread throughout the village.

At one of these concerts, the family of the wealthy Count Chodkiewicz listened intently. Impressed with this young man's talent, they took him to Kiev, a Russian city of great art and culture. In Kiev, Ignacy experienced his first concert. Until that point he had never heard a professional orchestra, a pianist, violinist, or even singer. After a week in the city, his love of music deepened. Upon his return, his father announced that Ignacy was about to embark on another adventure.

Chapter Two

A Musical Life Begins

On an autumn day in 1872, twelve-year-old Ignacy and his father arrived by train in the beautiful city of Warsaw. The Zamek, the ancient palace of the Polish kings, the wide Vistula River, and the crowded streets and parks excited him.

Ignacy was honored to be accepted at the Warsaw Conservatory, the same school where his idol, the Polish pianist and composer Fredrick Chopin, had studied.

Before returning to his job, Mr. Paderewski and his son journeyed to a large old house in Warsaw that served as the factory, shop, and living quarters of Kerntopf, the best piano manufacturer in town. The Kerntopfs invited Ignacy to live with them and their ten children. They also offered him the use of their excellent pianos.

It was difficult for Ignacy to say good-bye to his father, but he soon got used to life at the Kerntopfs and made friends at school. His quick movements, his pranks, and his golden-red hair earned him the nickname "The Squirrel." (Only red squirrels were found in Poland.)

Ignacy's first days in Warsaw seemed filled with promise, but his musical education didn't have a great start. Sadly, his first teacher at the conservatory told him that his hands were too small and his middle finger and thumb were too short to play the piano well. When his second teacher, Julian Janotha, praised his musical ability, Ignacy begged Professor Janotha to teach him the proper piano technique he had never learned. But, Professor Janotha felt he didn't need the fundamentals. Ignacy found another piano teacher on his own, but after his fourth lesson, he heard these words: "You will never be a pianist. Never."

His professors at the conservatory also didn't feel Ignacy had the potential to be a pianist, but they did feel he had the potential to be a composer. To prepare for this career, they urged him to learn as many instruments as possible.

Although Ignacy partially accepted their advice and learned the flute, oboe, clarinet, bassoon, horn, trumpet, and trombone, he wouldn't give up his dream of becoming a pianist. Despite discouraging words from his teachers, his clumsy finger work, and poor timing, he could take music he had never seen before, play the notes perfectly, and grasp the mood of the piece.

Between classes and practice sessions, Ignacy and his friends went sightseeing in and around Warsaw. For a boy who had loved reading about Polish history, he felt privileged to be at places he had only read about. He visited the Vilanov, the ornate summer palace of King John Sobieski, the Pole who had saved Western Europe by driving the Turks from Vienna. In the Palace Square, Ignacy admired the bronze figure of King Sigismond III, who in the 16th century had made Warsaw the Polish capital. The boy's deep admiration for Chopin took him a few miles outside of Warsaw to a one-story cottage where Chopin was born. These remnants of Poland's past reminded Ignacy of his commitment to Poland and music.

When Ignacy was fifteen years old, playing first trombone with the conservatory orchestra got him into a lot of trouble. Orchestra rehearsals interfered with his preparation for exams, and he wanted to use his time to study. His conductor demanded he attend rehearsals. Ignacy disagreed, and he was expelled. Protests from a majority of teachers at the conservatory earned Paderewski a pardon, and he returned.

A few months shy of his sixteenth birthday, Ignacy and two friends from the conservatory went on a musical tour without their parents knowing. This trio—a violinist, a cellist, and a pianist—hoped to find adventure and make some money as they traveled from town to town. After a short time on tour, one of the young musicians left, but Paderewski and his other friend, eighteen-year-old Ignacy Cielewicz, continued. They played in musty halls to sparse crowds and suffered through a harsh winter traveling in open carts and sleeping in cheap hotels. They stuffed old newspapers under their worn clothing to keep out the biting Russian winds. The boys finally wrote to their parents about their troubles and were ordered to come home. Ignacy Cielewicz went home immediately, but Ignacy Paderewski wanted to make another stop or two first.

Before he journeyed home, Ignacy loaned the money his father had sent him to an acquaintance from Warsaw who promised to return it in a few hours. The acquaintance turned out to be a thief, and the trusting Ignacy was left stranded without a penny. To make matters worse, someone had stolen Ignacy's luggage. Fortunately, an impoverished plumber that Ignacy met on the street offered the stranded teenager some bread and a place to stay.

Two weeks later a miracle happened: Mr. Paderewski dreamed that his son was in trouble in St. Petersburg. The desperate father wrote to the post office hoping to get in

Antonina Korsak Paderewska, Paderewski's first wife.

touch with Ignacy. Soon he was able to send him one hundred rubles.

After being reunited with his father, Ignacy returned to the conservatory. Working day and night, he finished a two-year program in six months. Mr. Paderewski proudly watched his son receive his diploma and play the Grieg *Concerto in A Minor* with the school orchestra.

After graduation, his dream of being a pianist was put on hold. Ignacy wanted to head to the famous musical centers of Berlin or Vienna to study piano, but he didn't have the money. He knew his father couldn't afford to pay his way so he remained in Warsaw and accepted a teaching position at the conservatory.

Early in 1880, at the age of nineteen, Ignacy married a beautiful girl named Antonina Korsak, a student at the conservatory. Antonina, who had the same first name as his sister, believed that her husband would become a famous pianist. The couple had little money but knew great happiness for a brief time. On October 1, 1880, their son, Alfred, was born. Antonina died nine days later. Suddenly, Paderewski had to face the future alone.

Chapter Three

Striving for Musical Perfection

Ignacy's infant son, the memory of Antonina and her dying wish that he continue his musical studies gave him strength. Ignacy knew he couldn't pursue their dream in Warsaw. He must journey to other cities, to centers of music, where he could learn more about his craft.

Entrusting his son, Alfred, in the care of his mother-in-law, Ignacy first traveled to Berlin, Germany, where he studied musical composition under the direction of Friedrich Kiel, a distinguished professor at the Royal Academy of Music. Ignacy soon became one of Kiel's star pupils.

In Berlin, Ignacy enjoyed meeting great composers, pianists, and conductors. He met Pablo de Sarasate and Joseph Joachim, famous violinists; and Anton Rubinstein and Richard Strauss, famous composers and pianists. He was also fortunate to have his own compositions published for fifty dollars—a generous amount of money at that time.

Although he personally received musical encouragement in Berlin and made many friends, Poles were often persecuted in Germany. Prejudice hurt, but it didn't destroy Ignacy's belief in himself or his love for his country.

When his money ran out in Berlin, he once again had to postpone his dream of becoming a pianist. He returned to

Warsaw. By day he taught piano at The Warsaw Conservatory; by night he studied Latin, math, literature, and history. His students and his friends at the conservatory wanted him to stay, but his goal wasn't to teach. He found teaching to be a very exhausting profession.

Early in 1884, the twenty-three-year-old Ignacy Jan Paderewski returned to Berlin to resume his musical studies. Before he left, he took Alfred to live with his father. The three year old's health worried Ignacy, and he wanted to provide Alfred with the best medical care. Although at that time doctors couldn't pinpoint what was wrong, today we know Alfred probably suffered from polio.

Returning to Berlin proved to be an important step in Ignacy's musical career. He studied with Professor Heinrich Urban, who gave him a solid foundation in orchestration (the arrangement of music for an orchestra.) Ignacy's drive and determination impressed Urban.

Taking a short break from his studies, Ignacy traveled to Poland's towering Tatra Mountains. There he met Madame Modjeska, a beautiful Polish actress, popular in both Poland and America. She loved Ignacy's music and his wit and charm. Later in her autobiography, Madame Modjeska recalled a premonition she had about him: "I knew he would make a name and fortune. His poetic face, combined with his genius, was bound to produce brilliant results."

That summer she encouraged this struggling musician to appear with her in the Polish town of Cracow. Modjeska's name was "magic" on the program, and her adoring fans filled the hall. After Modjeska beautifully recited Polish poetry, Ignacy played the piano. The audience applauded wildly. Madame Modjeska insisted he take the two-hundred-dollar profit from the performance and pursue his dream. "Poland needs you," Modjeska encouraged him.

"Every man and woman of Polish blood must fall in line. This one a soldier, that one as a nurse; the other as a writer; you as a musician."

Ignacy never forgot her advice, kindness, and support. Throughout his life he remembered how Modjeska had helped him to achieve his dream.

The money from his appearance with Modjeska enabled Ignacy to journey to another great musical city: Vienna, Austria. In Vienna he studied with Theodor Leschetizky, hailed as the second greatest piano teacher of the 19th century. (Karl Czerny, teacher of Franz Liszt was the first.) Leschetizky worked his pupils hard. He demanded they study one bar or phrase of a musical composition at a time, mastering fingering, pedaling, accent, and tone before attempting the next section. Ignacy longed to work with a teacher like this who had such high expectations. But Leschetizky's words, "You could have become a great pianist if you had only begun earlier," tortured Ignacy. He couldn't change the past. Nor would he abandon his dream just because as a young boy he hadn't had the opportunity to study properly.

Ignacy persevered, studied with Leschetizky, and learned from him. Leschetizky insisted on work, work, and more work, and Ignacy, who used to hide in treetops to avoid practice, delivered. When Leschetizky told him that his fingers lacked "discipline," Ignacy practiced finger exercises for hours. This talented professor so admired the young man's eagerness to learn that he never charged him for a single lesson. From Leschetizky, Ignacy learned that each finger creates emotion in playing: It does matter which finger plays a certain note.

One evening as Ignacy practiced in his candlelit apartment in Vienna, he noticed that a spider dangling from a

Paderewski in his early twenties.

silver thread seemed to be listening to a Chopin Etude in thirds. When Ignacy began another piece, this time in sixths, the spider hurried to the ceiling. As he resumed his study in thirds, the creature slid down its silver thread and rested on the piano, content and quiet. When Ignacy resumed his study in sixths, the spider returned to the ceiling. Down in thirds! Up to the ceiling in sixths! The daily visits of this spider with his eyes "so brilliant, like tiny, shining diamonds," fascinated Ignacy. One day when Ignacy returned from a short vacation, he discovered his tiny creature had vanished! The pianist never forgot the joy this musical spider brought to him during lonely hours of practice.

It was Leschetizky who arranged for Ignacy's first Vienna concert. The appreciative audiences encouraged him. Ignacy realized that in spite of years of discouragement he was finally going to be a pianist.

After success in Vienna, Ignacy spent eight months preparing for his Paris debut. In March 1888 at Paris' *Salle Erard*, a large enthusiastic crowd, which included the great Russian composer, Tchaikovsky, enjoyed musical selections performed by Paderewski. They included Beethoven's *Thirty-two Variations in C Minor* and the romantic Hungarian music of Listz's *Sixth Rhapsody*.

Audiences, hungry for more, invited Ignacy to give a second concert. This time he had only three weeks to prepare, but he worked day and night learning new selections. This new concert was a success. Due in part to his thick mane of reddish-gold hair, Paris critics affectionately called him "The Lion of Paris."

Paris marked the real beginning of Ignacy's life as an artist. There he experienced difficulties, disappointment, made mistakes, and nurtured hopes. He also met and

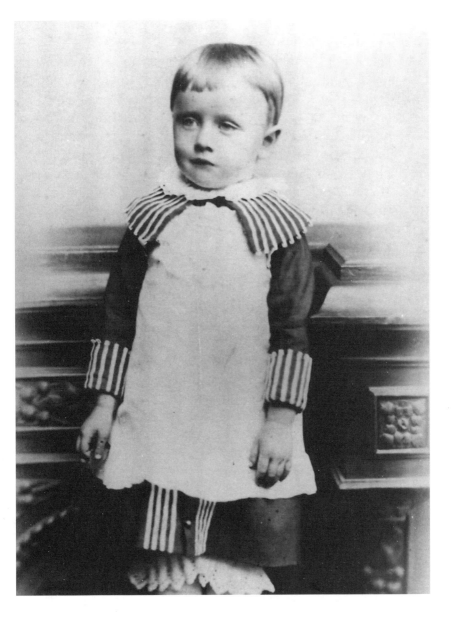

Alfred Paderewski at age three.

formed lasting friendships with the famous figures of the day in music, society, and politics.

He happily sent news of his success to his father, sister, and son, and soon brought Alfred to Paris to be near him. When Alfred felt strong enough, he was excited to attend some of his father's concerts. But when Alfred wasn't well enough to travel with his father to other cities and countries, Ignacy's good friends Mr. and Mrs. Wladyslaw Gorski and their son Wacio provided a loving home for Alfred in Paris.

After spending three seasons in Paris learning new programs and performing them for satisfied audiences, Ignacy wanted to conquer London. "My experience was my armor and technical skill my weapons," he explained.

When he arrived in London, he saw posters advertising his concert proclaiming, "Paderewski, the Lion of Paris." In Paris, the title had its place, but in London where he was an unknown, he felt it would seem as if he were showing off. He complained to Daniel Mayer, the manager who masterminded these posters, but the damage was already done. Nerves wracked the young pianist, and his first London concert didn't go well. Murmurs and whispers from the sparse audience destroyed his concentration. Critics made brutal comments. "Much noise, little music," *The Evening Standard* reported. *The Daily Telegraph* critic wrote, "Plainly we do not like Mr. Paderewski. The result of his labor may be marvelous, but it is not music." Ignacy cried after the concert and the criticism, but he wouldn't give up.

Attendance increased at his second concert, and this time the critics wrote positive reviews. By the end of the season, his concerts were sold out and most critics were enthusiastic. Although he didn't make a lot of money, Ignacy did cast a spell on his audiences with the beautiful tones and rhythms of his playing. When Ignacy Jan Paderewski per-

Theodore Leschetizky admired Paderewski's desire to learn.

formed, some felt they heard not one but several pianos playing at once. Others felt he made the piano sing and a human voice rise from it. Women in the audience rushed to the stage throwing flowers, trying to touch him and kiss his hands.

Many admired his beautiful blue deep-set eyes, high chiseled cheek bones, and his thick golden-red hair that often gave an appearance of a halo framing his head. In London, the great painter Edward Burne-Jones completed a sketch of Ignacy. It became one of his most famous drawings. Burne-Jones said of Ignacy, "How nice it must be to look as fine as one is inside."

During 1891, Ignacy performed for Queen Victoria at Windsor Castle. He triumphed at St. James's Hall. He played at private homes and became the center of attention at parties.

After his success in major European cities, he wondered what the future would hold across the Atlantic Ocean in America, the *new* world of artists.

Chapter Four

An American Welcome

On a rainy night in 1891, the steamship *Spray* sailed into New York harbor and brought Ignacy Jan Paderewski to America. A representative from the Steinway piano company greeted him: "We hear you have had brilliant successes in London and Paris, but let me tell you, Mr. Paderewski, you need not expect anything like that here in America." Upon hearing these biting words, Paderewski felt like taking the next steamer home, but he couldn't. He had a contract to honor and needed the thirty thousand dollars Steinway guaranteed for his American tour.

The Polish pianist made his American debut a few days later at New York's Carnegie Hall. Although he received mixed reviews, the public loved him immediately. Music critic Richard Aldrich reported that Paderewski "seemed to speak a new language in music; he raised its poetry, its magic, its mystery, its romantic eloquence, to a higher power than listeners knew. To every one of them, it seemed as if he spoke directly in an individual appeal, touching the heart as never before."

The thirty-one year-old Paderewski faced a grueling concert schedule: Eighty performances with very little time off—a difficult feat for a pianist. He argued that he needed time off between performances to practice, mentally prepare for the next concert, and rest his hands. But since it was too late to change the schedule, he tackled this difficult agenda.

Where could he practice? At his hotel, the manager warned him that the practice sessions would disturb the guests. One night Paderewski and his secretary, Hugo Goerlitz, stole away to the Steinway piano warehouse on Fourteenth Street. The glow of two candles offered light, and the dedicated pianist practiced until morning, accompanied by the snores of Hugo Goerlitz and the warehouse's night watchman.

After successful New York concerts, Paderewski traveled about America, dazzling audiences in Boston, Chicago, and Milwaukee. Fans packed concert halls and begged for encores. Often after playing two or three hours during the concert, he'd play an extra hour as an encore! Paderewski's finger work and understanding of the musical selections impressed his listeners. One review stated: "his fingers glide over the keyboards as if it were all done by electricity." In Portland, Maine, one thousand people crowded around just to shake his hand. Paderewski felt a special loyalty to his fans so he obliged every one, and his hand swelled to twice its size!

Paderewski was a perfectionist. He wouldn't rely on his talent alone. At that time he worked seventeen hours a day. His arms and hands were very tired, and the Steinway piano he used caused him discomfort. He later said, ". . . the actual physical strength required to produce a very big tone from a Steinway, as it was then, was almost beyond the power of any artist. The strain was terrific." The Erard piano he played on in Europe was much lighter to the touch.

He convinced the piano regulator to make special adjustments to the Steinway piano so it wouldn't sap as much of

Polish Pianist and Patriot

Steinway Hall,

New York,

November 10, 1891.

Mr. Charles F. Tretbar takes much pleasure in inviting you to be present at the First of the Inaugural Concerts in America of Ignace J. Paderewski which will occur on Tuesday Evening, Nov. 17, 1891, at the Music Hall (57th St. and 7th Ave.). You can obtain upon presentation of this note of invitation, to the Ticket Seller at the Box Office of the Hall (57th St. and 7th Ave.), _____ Reserved Seat Tickets, on and after Thursday A. M., Nov. 12, until Monday Afternoon, Nov. 16, at Five (5) o'clock, when the privilege of acceptance will positively expire.

A ticket from Paderewski's debut concert in America.

his strength. For a time Paderewski noted an improvement. But at one concert near the end of his tour, as he struck the opening cords of Beethoven's *Appassionata*, he felt something snap in his right arm. Unbearable pain gripped him! He thought he would have to leave the stage. But, somehow he forced himself to continue. The audience, unaware that Paderewski had almost fainted from the pain, enjoyed the performance. Later, Paderewski learned that another piano regulator, unfamiliar with Paderewski's wishes, had made an incorrect adjustment to the piano without telling him. As a result of this mistake, Paderewski seriously tore and strained some tendons in his right arm and injured his fourth finger.

"There is nothing I can do for you. You must rest," the dcctor advised. But Paderewski couldn't. When questioned why he would still play when he was injured, he responded, "I may never come this way again." At another time in his career, the keyboard was bathed in blood when Paderewski played too soon after an operation on his finger.

His eighty-performance tour was so successful that audiences demanded more concerts. Mr. Steinway offered Paderewski an additional twenty-seven concerts and promised more profits. During the first eighty sell-out concerts, most of the profits went to agents—not to Paderewski. Now, a dilemma confronted him: Should he decline Mr. Steinway's generous offer and try to recover from his injuries, or should he accept and risk further injury? He had a lot of expenses, including sending money home to his sister and elderly father and paying for Alfred's medical care. He performed.

At the end of Paderewski's first successful American tour of 107 concerts in 117 days, Mr. Tretbar, the man who had greeted him so coldly on his arrival, apologized to

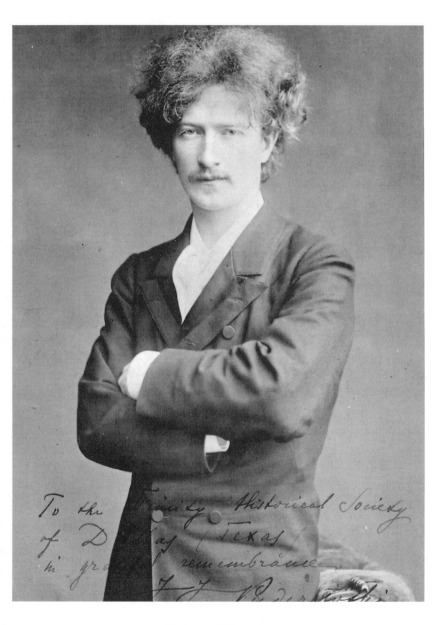

Paderewski in 1891.

Paderewski and expressed his admiration for him. Tretbar's sincere words were a joy to Paderewski, and the two developed a lasting friendship.

Paderewski returned to America the following year. During his second tour he gave sixty-seven concerts in twenty-seven American cities. He developed a deep affection for America. In his lifetime he appeared in over two hundred American cities presenting over fifteen hundred concerts to adoring fans.

On most of his American visits, Paderewski toured America in a unique way. Steinway rented a private railroad car for him. It was soon equipped with an upright piano, and Paderewski's piano tuner traveled with him. Paderewski enjoyed this mode of travel: His car provided sleeping quarters, a place to enjoy his meals prepared by his Pullman chef, and a place to play cards and to practice for his performance. Workers in the railway yards were treated to free concerts as they listened to Paderewski practice in his train as it rested on the sidetracks. Some people felt honored just to see his train pass by.

"Paddy," as he was affectionately called in America, became a star. His pictures appeared in store windows. Reporters wanted to interview him. Stories appeared in gossip columns. Women tried to snip pieces of his hair. His fans sought autographs and cheered loudly. Many wealthy families wanted him as a dinner guest, hopeful that he might play in their homes.

Often a guest at the New York City home of poet and *Century* magazine editor Richard Watson Gilder, Paderewski enjoyed the laughter of Gilder's five delightful children and the company of such notable authors as Mark Twain and Rudyard Kipling. He met financial giants like Andrew Carnegie and John D. Rockefeller, Jr. and admired

An autographed musical quote from Paderewski to a young fan.

the civic duty and responsibility they showed. They made millions of dollars, but they also contributed a portion of their wealth to others. He, too, would eventually make a fortune and use much of it to help others.

Once when Paderewski was still a struggling musician, he was refused admission to a concert he had traveled miles to see. He never forgot his disappointment. As a result, he never refused those who wanted to hear his concerts but couldn't get tickets. If there weren't seats available, Paderewski made sure that his fans could be somewhere in the hall, even if it meant some had to stand in a corner. They were grateful, for his beautiful performance traveled to the corners of the hall, too.

Paderewski didn't let success blind him from seeing other people's needs and helping them. When he heard that an order of cloistered nuns couldn't hear his concert, he quietly went to them and gave a private recital. He donated ten thousand dollars to establish the Paderewski Award, a fund that offered cash prizes to talented American composers who were "struggling for recognition or encouragement."

He responded quickly to a newspaper account about a poor Polish couple from Baltimore. The husband had been killed by a train, and the man's wife gave birth prematurely to their child when she heard of her husband's death. Paderewski visited the widow and her newborn child in the hospital and arranged for lifetime financial care for them.

Paderewski gave many benefit concerts. One raised forty-five hundred dollars towards the building of New York City's Washington Centennial Arch at the foot of Fifth Avenue. As a memento, his friend Richard Watson Gilder carved the initial "P" into the top of the monument. Gilder wrote to him: "Our own initials were carved on the hidden parts of these stones, and a large P for Paderewski took its place among the rest. So your initial is built into the very structure of the monument, and as long as the history of the arch is remembered, your generous deed will be kept in mind."

On another American tour in the city of San Jose, California, Paderewski showed kindness toward two Stanford University students who sponsored one of his concerts. The students made a mistake by scheduling a concert during Holy Week. Attendance was poor. The two students went to Paderewski for help. He did not want to see struggling students go into debt so he accepted whatever they could afford to pay, which turned out to be only half of what he had been promised. One of these young men was Herbert Hoover, who years later, as head of the American Relief Administration, sent food, clothing, and medical supplies to a starving Poland. In 1929, Herbert Hoover became the thirty-first president of the United States.

During each visit, the bonds between Paderewski and America strengthened. It was a relationship that would have both historical and personal importance.

Chapter Five

Paderewski and the World

The name Paderewski spread throughout America and the world.

Long lines formed at the box office when Paderewski concert tickets went on sale. "Sold-out" signs appeared quickly. On the night of each performance, large crowds gathered outside the concert hall hoping to purchase tickets from a "scalper" or catch a glimpse of the handsome musician's arrival or departure.

Inside, an enthusiastic crowd warmly welcomed "Paddy." The tuxedo-dressed pianist took his seat at the grand piano. Dim lighting enveloped the stage, and silence fell over the hall, a silence Paderewski demanded. If someone chose to talk or shuffle a program during a Paderewski concert, Paderewski stopped until silence returned. "I play only before audiences who listen to music and not their own talking," he once commented. Often his eyes were shut tightly as his small, strong hands ran over the keyboard, bringing life to the compositions of well-known composers. Occasionally, he performed one of his original works. After the final notes of his performances, the hall exploded with applause and "bravos."

Between 1891 and 1914, Paderewski toured America many times. He toured practically every country in Europe, including Poland, France, Italy, Ireland, Belgium, and

Russia. He performed in Australia, South Africa, and South America. In addition to the universal language of music, Paderewski spoke eloquently in Polish, Russian, English, French, German, Italian, and Spanish. This ability to speak to so many in their native language impressed audiences. Heads of state invited him to dinner, and lavish parties were held in his honor. He played at the White House. All of these opportunities later served him well as a statesman.

As he toured the world, he learned the art of government and diplomacy. He informed all who would listen of Poland's struggle to get the divided pieces of her country back. His knowledge of world issues and concern for his country impressed many who met him.

When Paderewski wasn't on tour, he needed a place to call home. He loved Poland and bought property there, but was forced to sell it because at this point in his life living there proved difficult. He needed a location that was a convenient base for tours and close to specialists for his son, who was confined to a wheelchair.

A villa named Riond-Bosson, near the little town of Morges in Switzerland, became an ideal location for Paderewski's home base. Built during the French Revolution, it towered several stories high. Large balconies offered a beautiful view of the Swiss Alps. At Riond-Bosson, Paderewski rested, composed, and prepared himself for his tours. He and Alfred discussed literature, played chess, and wrote comedies to entertain the many guests who were welcome at their beautiful estate.

In May 1899, Paderewski married Helena Gorska, the woman who cared for Alfred. She had been married to Paderewski's violinist friend, Mr. Gorski, but their marriage was unhappy. When Helena's annulment of her first marriage was finally granted, Helena and Ignacy Jan

Paderewski were married at the historic Cathedral of St. John in Warsaw, Poland. Madame Padereska traveled with Paderewski, and she was his loyal companion. They were devoted to each other and shared a love for Alfred, music, and Poland.

But, sadness soon came to Riond-Bosson. While Paderewski performed in Spain, Alfred, then twenty years old, journeyed to a specialist in Augsburg. On the trip, Alfred caught a cold and died of pneumonia.

To deal with Alfred's death, Paderewski immersed himself in work. He put finishing touches on his opera *Manru,* which he had begun seven years earlier.

Riond-Bosson and a nearby farm became a haven for Paderewski. Parrots and cockatoos, horses, squirrels, rabbits, goats, and ducks were important residents. Paderewski enjoyed his flock of sheep, a gift from Edward VII of England, and Madame Paderewska's poultry yard, filled with over a thousand chickens. Dozens of dogs, including St. Bernards and Pekinese, freely roamed the property. At one point, Paderewski insisted that his godchild's cocker spaniel, Macius, be brought to Riond-Bosson while the family visited him there. "When you have an animal in your care, you take him with you. You don't leave him behind," he explained.

Guests were always welcome, and Paderewski treated them to beautiful music on one of Riond-Bosson's seven pianos. He loved entertaining at picnics and dinner parties presided over by his wife and sister, Antonina, who came to live with him when her husband died. He was a playful host. His favorite prank involved placing a dummy made of stuffed pillows and stockings under the covers of a guest bed and hiding behind the door to observe his guest's reaction!

One special guest at Riond-Bosson was a wonderful

Madame Paderewska in 1904.

green parrot Paderewski acquired in Australia called Cockey Roberts. When pelting rain postponed Paderewski's sightseeing trip, his Australian manager brought in Cockey Roberts to entertain him. Cockey Roberts' shrill voice cursed, swore, and offered, "Look here, have a drink—have a drink." The vocabulary and antics of this bird so delighted the Paderewskis that they kept him. Cockey Roberts toured Australia, New Zealand, Tasmania, and America with the Paderewskis and even had his own room at Riond-Bosson!

During practice, Paderewski purposely closed the doors to tease the bird, but the parrot refused to be shut out and knocked on the door with his beak. Paderewski pretended to be very quiet. Cockey Roberts knocked again and Paderewski called out, "Who is there? Who is it?"

An angry voice replied, "Cockey Roberts!"

"Who?" Paderewski asked, pretending not to understand.

"COCKEY ROBERTS! COCKEY ROBERTS!" the parrot shrieked.

Paderewski opened the doors and in strutted the parrot heading straight for the piano. As the musician played, Cockey Roberts perched on Paderewski's foot for hours, occasionally exclaiming, "Oh, Lord, how beautiful!"

In addition to being an animal lover, Paderewski was an environmentalist. When Paderewski heard of his neighbor's plan to cut down a beautiful stand of trees near his property, the musician offered money to save them. The neighbor asked an exorbitant price, but Paderewski paid to save the trees.

Amid the beauty and peace of his properties, he found time to compose. In his second-floor music room, he created fine musical compositions, including his *Piano Sonata*,

Riond-Bosson, Morges Switzerland.

his third set of *Variations*, and his famous *Symphony in B Minor* Op.24, a patriotic tribute to Poland.

In between productive times at Riond-Bosson came the hectic concert tours. A combination of factors, both physical and emotional, took its toll on Paderewski at the height of his career. Long hours of practice and little rest drained him. As he lay awake at night, he mentally rehearsed his program, note for note.

In 1905, a train accident in America threw Paderewski against the table in his dining car, injuring a muscle in the back of his neck and causing him great pain for years. He began to look at the piano as an enemy to avoid. "Something was happening to my nerves that made me completely hate the piano . . . no matter what I played, I did not feel in touch with the instrument. It was a kind of torture . . . The easiest piece in my repertoire I could not manage. The touch was strange to me."

Doctors ordered complete rest, but Paderewski found it difficult to slow down. He needed money to finance his donations to patriotic projects and the needy in Poland and around the world. He gave money to anyone who asked for it and to many who didn't. When he met an eleven-year-old boy in London who showed great promise as a pianist, he gave the boy money to go to Vienna and study with his former teacher, the famous Professor Leschetizky. In his lifetime Paderewski gave away millions of dollars.

In 1909, pain again forced Paderewski to stop a tour and return to Europe for treatments. In his time away from the piano, he began to devote his energy to another childhood dream. Since he was ten years old, he had wanted to honor the great Polish victory against the Teutonic Knights at Grunwald that took place in 1410. As a boy, he carefully calculated that he would donate the monument on July 15,

An autographed card by Paderewski.

1910, the 500th anniversary of this famous battle for Polish freedom. He began saving.

On a warm day in July in 1910, Paderewski, four months shy of his fiftieth birthday, journeyed to Cracow (Austrian Poland) to witness the dedication of a beautiful granite and bronze sculpture designed by Antoni Wiwulski, a talented young Polish sculptor.

Proud that he had fulfilled his dream, Paderewski spoke in front of the huge crowds that packed the square and overflowed into the nearby streets. Russian and Prussian agents mingled among the spectators, carefully listening to Ignacy Jan's words of prophecy for future independence: ". . . The achievement upon which we look today was not born of hatred, but out of deep love for our native land; not because of her present helpless state, but because of a vision of her bright and powerful future."

Paderewski had often heard thunderous applause for his playing; now he heard it for his speechmaking. His roles as a public speaker and a political activist were developing.

That same year of 1910, he journeyed to Lwow for a belated celebration of the hundredth anniversary of Chopin's birth. Paderewski had been invited to play at this tribute to his boyhood hero, but he knew he couldn't play well. The neuritis (nerve damage) in his hands was too severe. He gave the place of honor to Ernest Schelling, his American pupil. Although he couldn't pay tribute to Chopin through music that day, Paderewski did honor the memory of Chopin by delivering a moving speech in which he announced of Poland, ". . . the nation cannot perish that has a soul so great, so immortal." These were bold words considering there were some enemies of Poland scattered throughout the audience, enemies who did not want to see Poland reunited.

These two speeches in 1910 prepared him for a new and unexpected career. The Polish people, who still longed for their country to be reunited, saw Paderewski as a leader. He won their trust and respect.

It would be several more years before he would enter the political world. In the meantime, he resumed his concert tours. Pain in his arm and fingers still troubled him. At one point the musician Sir Henry Heymann advised him to go at once to Paso Robles for mud bath treatments. So Paderewski went to this peaceful California town for three weeks of treatment. The mud and mineral baths at the Hotel El Paso de Robles relieved his neuritis, and he continued his concert tour in comfort. In February 1914, Paderewski bought a ranch in Paso Robles where he planted acres of almond, walnut, and prune trees and vineyards. This property, too, would be another haven, like Riond-Bosson.

During the summer of 1914, fear gripped all of Europe after the assassination of Austrian Archduke Francis Ferdinand on June 28, by a Serbian nationalist. Soon the world would be at war. The tragic events that were about to unfold created a new role for Ignacy Jan Paderewski.

Chapter Six

World War I

In boyhood games, Paderewski had played soldier. During World War I, he would battle for Poland, armed with his powerful words. Poland was still not recognized as a country on a world map, but Poland was still a country to those who loved her. The Polish spirit had not been broken.

Paderewski realized Poland's geographic location made her one of the greatest battlefields of the war. He stated that Poland, ". . . lay between the territories of the belligerents who sought one another's throats." No matter which side attacked, these enemies left death and destruction. They destroyed homes and farms. They robbed the peasants of more than two million cattle and one million horses. Agriculture and industry were destroyed. Every part of Poland knew blood and starvation. Paderewski wept at the news that some of his countrymen survived by eating roots and tree bark.

Because Poland was divided and ruled by three countries, Polish men and boys were forced to fight each other on their own land. This haunted Paderewski. His friend, Nobel-prize winning Polish author Henryk Sienkiewicz, wrote, "It frequently happens that when the Red Cross go out to collect the wounded from a battlefield they lift from one heap one man in German uniform, another in Austrian, and a third in Russian uniform and discover that they are all Poles."

During the early months of the war, Paderewski spent time in and around Riond-Bosson discussing Poland's predicament with other interested individuals. Paderewski believed that this terrible war, which would eventually involve as many as thirty nations, would help the Poles recover their divided land and put Poland back on the map of Europe. It could happen with an Allied victory, but it wouldn't happen overnight. It wouldn't happen without great suffering.

Paderewski helped organize relief committees in Vevey (Switzerland), Paris, and London which provided food, shelter, clothing, and medicine for Poland. But he knew he must journey to America for more help.

Believing in America's goodness and sense of justice, he arrived in America in the spring of 1915 with three important goals to accomplish: raise money for relief work, make Americans aware of Poland's needs, and organize the different Polish-American organizations into a unified front.

Although Paderewski hated asking for money, he did so for the sake of his country and earned the title of "international beggar." In addition, he used at least two million dollars of his own. His wife opened a craft shop in Paris where artists made dolls dressed in traditional Polish costumes. Proceeds from the sale of these dolls at Paderewski's concerts kept many war victims from starvation and death.

Over the years, Paderewski had made influential friends. Now he called upon some for help, including Thomas Alva Edison, Mrs. John Wanamaker, and former President William Howard Taft. He persuaded Taft to become chairman of his Polish Relief Committee. Australia's opera star, Nellie Melba, donated sixty-five thousand dollars to Paderewski's cause.

In San Francisco, Paderewski launched a unique concert-speech tour. Standing on a stage in front of a backdrop of a Polish flag that stretched ceiling to floor, the fifty-four-year-old musician eloquently described his country's suffering. After his inspiring speech, he played the music of Chopin. Audiences spread Poland's good name. Donors wrote out generous checks.

During World War I, Paderewski visited every state and gave over three hundred concert-speeches. He made great progress, but he knew that to effectively represent Poland's voice in America, he had to speak to the president of the United States.

One day in the fall of 1915, Paderewski spotted a newspaper photograph of President Woodrow Wilson's close friend and trusted advisor, Colonel Edward House. Paderewski soon met House, and they became friends. Colonel House arranged for Paderewski to attend a White House dinner. After the meal, Paderewski played Chopin for President Wilson and spoke of Poland's needs. Wilson listened attentively to Paderewski's views. Paderewski's influence in government circles was becoming well-known. The German Embassy reported to Berlin that the United States was well-informed of Poland's situation because of Paderewski's activities.

On November 5, 1916, in the Proclamation of the Two Emperors, Germany made a tempting offer: Germany promised that after the war Germany and Austria would take all the land conquered from Russia and turn it into a new Poland. They would do so, but the Poles had to join Germany's side in the war. Although some Poles saw hope in this proclamation, Paderewski saw right through this offer. He knew it was Germany's trick to make the Allies believe there was no longer a Polish "cause" to fight for and to get the Poles to join their army. On behalf of the Poles,

Paderewski was deeply troubled by the suffering of his country.

Paderewski responded in a written protest against this German promise of independence. He emphasized that this offer came from countries who "having stripped Poland of her robes, now offered her rags in return for the last drops of her blood." The next day, President Wilson assured Paderewski that Poland would exist again.

In the opening days of 1917, after two and one half years of bitter fighting, Europe suffered terrible destruction and Poland's lands were devastated. Could Paderewski's country endure much more? Paderewski knew if the United States entered the war, Poland's cause would gain strength. As President Wilson formulated his new view of Eastern Europe after the war—a Europe where nations would dedicate themselves to freedom and brotherhood—Colonel House knew it was time to present President Wilson with a detailed study of Poland's situation. Respecting Paderewski's knowledge and insight, Colonel House turned to him.

Paderewski obliged and labored to prepare a report for the president. His ideas were used in President Wilson's address to the Senate. "I take it for granted that statesmen everywhere are agreed that there should be a united, independent, and autonomous Poland." Wilson's speech gave Poles around the world reason to be grateful.

In the late winter and early spring of 1917, events happened that convinced Wilson that America must enter the war: He learned of a German plot to involve Mexico in war with the United States. German submarines were sinking American ships. The United States declared war on Germany on April 6, 1917, with Polish independence as one of its aims.

Paderewski and Poland rejoiced. Poland's rebirth could become a reality. Paderewski had seized every opportunity

Bombings during World War I destroyed much of Poland.

to make people aware of his beloved Poland. He had convinced "countless numbers of Americans of the justice of
the course Wilson was going to take."

As Americans prepared to fight, Paderewski had another
concern. Poland didn't have an army. Paderewski believed
that an independent Polish army that fought side-by-side
with the Allies would boldly show the world Poland did
exist. He repeatedly sought permission from the United
States government to recruit Poles in America who weren't
subject to the draft. Although he was told "no" many times,
he finally got permission to recruit Poles who were not
United States citizens and who hadn't yet applied for
United States citizenship. These recruits formed an army
called the Kosciuszko Division, named after Thaddeus
Kosciuszko, the great Polish general who had fought for
America's independence with George Washington.

When Paderewski recruited, he passed out copies of the
patriotic poems of Adam Mickiewicz, a Polish poet. He also
composed a War Hymn for his volunteers.

After months and months of planning on Paderewski's
part, the Kosciuszko Division finally arrived in Europe.
Joined by more forces in Europe, this division became one-
hundred-thousand strong. Poland's brilliant general, Josef
Haller led these men on the side of the Allies under the once
forbidden Polish flag. At daily roll call, the name Ignacy
Jan Paderewski was shouted out by a hundred thousand soldiers to honor the pianist who had done so much.

On January 8, 1918, one year after Paderewski had prepared his famous memorandum for Colonel House and
almost four years since World War I began, President
Wilson addressed the joint session of Congress. He presented his Fourteen Points—his program for world peace.
His Thirteenth Point advocated Poland's independent political status and her "free and secure access to the sea."

Sample of Paderewski's written gratitude, Polish Victim's Relief Fund letterhead.

Soon, through the help of Americans, the Allies handed defeat after defeat to the Central Powers. One by one they surrendered. World War I ended on November 11, 1918, about nineteen months after the United States had entered the war, and less than a year after Wilson had stated his Fourteen Points. On that historic day in Warsaw, Poland, war-weary citizens cried and young children eagerly disarmed German soldiers, taking away their weapons and helmets.

Paderewski's work in the United States was completed. In his four-year struggle, he accomplished the goals he journeyed to America to achieve. Through his persistence, he helped to save his beloved country from her foreign enemies. Could he do anything now to help Poland retrieve its stolen lands and unite its people? He would set out for Europe to try.

Chapter Seven

Leading Poland

Even though the official fighting of World War I had stopped, hatreds still existed. This nightmarish war, which had lasted fifty-one months, had claimed over twenty million lives and over twenty-one million wounded. Much healing had to take place.

As world leaders scheduled a peace conference to open in Paris in January 1919, Paderewski knew he too should be in Europe where Poland's future would be determined.

World War I had made it possible for Poland to once again exist as a nation. But, many obstacles still stood in her way to freedom. Poland needed a government the Allies would recognize. If Poland had such a government, then the Allies would send in supplies and allow Poland's voice to be heard at the upcoming peace conference.

In reality, Poland had a government headed by General Josef Pilsudski, a Polish war hero. Although Pilsudski was a hero to some of the Poles, to the Allies, Pilsudski was the unknown, and they feared him. They needed someone in charge whom they could trust. The Allies trusted Paderewski.

Lord Balfour, foreign secretary of Great Britain and close friend of Paderewski, urged him, "you must go there and unite all the parties." Paderewski agreed to go to Poland, but only on the condition the British send him to

Poland in a British warship. Arriving in this official manner would clearly show to Pilsudski that Paderewski had British support.

The H.M.S. *Concord*, a British Royal Navy warship, traveled through the freezing waters of the Baltic, avoiding the booby-trapped mines set during the war. On Christmas Eve their famous passenger, Paderewski, entertained the captain and the officers for several hours on a battered piano in the wardroom. The crew couldn't believe the excellent music Paderewski produced even though he suffered from a bad cold and several piano keys were missing.

On Christmas Day the *Concord* sailed into the port of Danzig, (today known as Gdansk). In Danzig, red flags of the German Revolutionary Council were an ominous reminder to Paderewski that all Poland's troubles with Germany weren't over. Danger lay ahead.

Paderewski boarded a train for Poznan, his next stop in Poland. German officers stormed aboard, warning Paderewski to stay out of Poznan, still a German city. After British officers, who accompanied Paderewski, threatened the German soldiers, the train proceeded. When their train finally reached Poznan, Paderewski welcomed the new sight of Polish, French, and British flags decorating the train station. Grateful Poles, happy to see Paderewski, led him in a torchlight procession.

Paderewski fell ill with bronchitis. Two days later on December 27, as ten thousand school children marched passed his hotel to pay tribute to him, German soldiers opened fire on the peaceful march with explosive and dum-dum bullets. Children ran for safety. Windows shattered. A bullet pierced the wall directly above Paderewski's bed. Madame Paderewska later wrote to a friend, "If my husband felt any fear, he did not show it."

As Paderewski left Poznan for Warsaw, cheering crowds stopped his train. For four years he had been their hope for survival. Now he was with them to help them rebuild. Paderewski made over seventeen speeches during this triumphal procession.

Upon his arrival in Warsaw, a hundred thousand people filled the snow-covered streets. Aniela Strakacz, an eyewitness who later became a dear friend of the Paderewski's, recorded in her journal: "Suddenly, a murmur rose from the crowd and grew to a crescendo of cries, 'He's here!'... a mighty roar went up: 'Long Live Paderewski!' 'Long Live Wilson!' 'Long Live America!'" Some members of the crowd unharnessed the horses from Paderewski's carriage and pulled it all the way to the Hotel Bristol.

Paderewski met with Pilsudski, urging him to form a representative coalition government immediately. He told him it would be Poland's only way to get help from the Allies. After two hours of discussion, they failed to reach an agreement.

Disappointed, Paderewski quickly left for Cracow, the former Polish capital. Eventually, Pilsudski reconsidered his decision and sent one of his Generals to Cracow to bring Paderewski back. Pilsudski and Paderewski, who had disagreements with each other, united for Poland's sake. They held Poland together during the critical moments of 1919.

On January 22, 1919, Ignacy Jan Paderewski became premier of Poland, although Pilsudski was still chief of state and had authority over Paderewski.

On January 26, 1919, thousands of Polish citizens, dressed in rags and barefooted, waited in the snow to cast a ballot. It had been well over one hundred years since Poles were able to vote for their own representative.

From left to right, Paderewski with Herbert Hoover, Josef Pilsudski and Polish officers in 1919 in Warsaw, Poland.

Fifteen days later, on February 10, the first Sejm, the Polish legislature, opened. Paderewski, who as a little boy had wanted to help his country, now spoke to the first sovereign Polish parliament since the end of the eighteenth century. Paderewski's words, promising hope for Poland, brought tears and a standing ovation.

Soon the United States officially recognized the new Polish government, and France, Great Britain, and Italy gave their approval. Poland was again ready to take its place in world affairs.

After Paderewski succeeded in making the Polish government acceptable to the Allies, he had to help rebuild a broken country and help the three separate parts of Poland work together. It was a difficult task. Different currencies in circulation and different legal systems hampered unification.

Eleven million acres of farmland and six million acres of forests were in ruin. Millions of farm animals had to be brought in to replace those stolen or slaughtered during the war. Homes in cities and villages were in shambles. The transportation system had been disrupted. The German army had blown up 7,500 bridges and 940 railways. Roads had been destroyed; there were few cars left to drive.

Influenza, typhoid and starvation crippled the population. It was reported that there were no dogs and only a few cats left in Poland—all the rest had been eaten. Paderewski had used his own private funds to help out the Polish White Cross, an organization started by Madame Paderewska to help Poland's impoverished citizens.

Years earlier, Paderewski had helped Herbert Hoover, a student at Stanford. Now Hoover, administrator of the American Food Mission, cut through red tape and promptly sent food, medicine, clothing, and expert advisors to help

Poland survive and rebuild. Paderewski worked closely with him.

Paderewski had two roles to play: Premier of a country rising from the ashes of war, and Poland's chief delegate at the Paris Peace Conference. Paderewski had to juggle his time between Poland and Paris in 1919. There was no time for his music. One author observed, "He seldom if ever spoke of it (music), but it was frequently noticed by friends that when he was seated alone at his desk or engaged in conversation his fingers moved on the arm of his chair or on the table's edge as if he were running an imaginary scale on the keyboard."

Paderewski stayed up way past midnight pouring over letters and documents, using his photographic memory to store names, facts and figures. He took time to meet with individual citizens who wanted to talk to him, he attended cabinet meetings, and often smoothed over rough situations when government officials disagreed. While Paderewski dealt with problems at home, Poland's second delegate to the Peace Conference, Roman Dmowski, spent his time in Paris at the Peace Conference presenting Poland's claims to the chief delegates. Although Dmowski gave a remarkable speech, he didn't gain their sympathy.

Paderewski, the chief delegate from Poland, arrived just in time to restate Dmowski's claims for Poland. The delegates especially admired Paderewski's knowledge of European history and his ability to see another's point of view. They were impressed that he didn't need an interpreter and respected his negotiating skills.

Although Paderewski made a favorable impression, these exceptional qualities didn't further his cause. On June 28, 1919, at the Palace of Versailles in the Great Hall of Mirrors, Paderewski signed the Treaty of Versailles for

Poland. On the positive side, the treaty recognized Poland's independence and gave Poland some of her lands back from Austria and Germany. It also offered Poland free access to the Baltic Sea through a strip of land known as the Polish Corridor.

On the negative side, Paderewski knew there were no great victories for Poland. Even after his eloquent pleas, only a portion of Poland's frontiers were definitely established. The port city of Danzig that Paderewski had entered that Christmas Day wasn't given to Poland, but was made a free state under the League of Nations' supervision (the organization designed to make the peace secure.) Paderewski, who was often intuitive when it came to his country, knew real trouble lay ahead with that decision.

Under the circumstances, Poland had little choice. If Poland rejected the Versailles Treaty, the Allies would abandon the Poles. Then Poland would be left to negotiate with the Germans on their own. Since this setup spelled danger for Poland, they signed. On July 31, the Polish Sejm ratified the Treaty of Versailles.

Some Poles who blamed Paderewski for Poland's failure to get everything she asked for at the Peace Conference failed to realize that negotiating the peace is often far more difficult than winning the war. When the attacks began, Paderewski was sensitive to criticism and it troubled him.

Paderewski's critics also said he was a poor financial manager. Others resented that he brought in foreigners to solve some of Poland's problems. They viewed his move into the royal castle, which had always been the seat of government as well as the royal residence, as a sign he viewed himself as a king. When Madame Paderewska intercepted messages to spare her husband from dealing with them or interrupted cabinet meetings, rumors began to circulate that she was running the government. Some made fun of her. These negative comments hurt Paderewski because he adored his wife and knew of all the good she did for Poland's needy.

More internal trouble brewed in Poland, and different party factions argued in the Sejm. There were attempts on Paderewski's life, others called for his resignation. At first, not being a member of a political party worked to Paderewski's advantage, but now it proved to be a disadvantage for he had no party to support him when the attacks came.

Although Paderewski still had his loyal supporters, he felt he didn't have the majority backing him. Others had their own visions of how to rebuild Poland. Since Paderewski refused to harm Poland's chances for democracy, he resigned as premier of Poland a little less than a year after he had accepted that office.

Sadness colored the end of his premiership of Poland. That Christmas of 1919 was an unhappy one. A weary Paderewski concentrated on his failure, for it was hard for him at that moment to realize that he had served his country well.

Chapter Eight

The Years Between Wars

In February of 1920, two months after his resignation as premier of Poland, Paderewski left Warsaw and returned to Riond-Bosson. Sunshine and crowds of well-wishers greeted him.

His final days as Poland's premier still troubled him, but Paderewski had little time to dwell on his problems. When Russia invaded Poland during the summer of 1920, he put Poland's interests above his own disappointment, and begged the Allies for help once again. Because the Allies respected Paderewski, they sent arms, money, and military advisors, enabling the Poles to resist the Russians.

Paderewski also willingly represented Poland at the League of Nations and the Conference of Ambassadors. Aniela Strakacz, wife of Paderewski's personal secretary, Sylwin Strakacz, remembered Paderewski's speech to some of the world's greatest diplomats and a packed house of spectators at a December 4, 1920, meeting of the League of Nations, "For more than an hour Paderewski addressed this group in French without notes and held them spellbound as if he were playing Chopin for them." Eventually, Paderewski resigned both posts when he realized these organizations were powerless and unable to achieve their

Paderewski and Helena with the Chief of Council of American Indians in Paso Robles Park.

goals. Poland continued to fight off attacks from neighboring countries and struggled to establish its borders.

At the end of 1920, Paderewski's lifetime savings were gone. He had even borrowed additional money to fund charities he and Madame Paderewska believed in, and now had to pay those debts. At age sixty, he'd have to return to the concert circuit to earn more money. With the exception of his wartime benefit concerts for Poland, he hadn't played for five years. Returning to the concert stage required much preparation, but he accepted the challenge and began with a trip to America to renew himself and restore his strength.

He arrived in New York on Feb. 13, 1921, to crowds of well-wishers, photographers, and reporters and soon journeyed to Paso Robles, California, for a much-needed rest.

Aniela Strakacz remembered the concert pianist's Paso Robles welcome: "The car with the Paderewskis in it inched along between a guard of honor consisting of two rows of automobiles, in military formation, filled with people holding flaming torches that turned night into day. Small children walked backward in front of the slowly moving car and strewed the ground with flowers."

Paderewski spent several weeks in Paso Robles. He stayed at the Hotel El Paso de Robles and took advantage of the soothing mud and mineral baths and enjoyed breakfasts of boiled herring, bread, and strong coffee. He enjoyed long walks in the hills and admired the stately oaks and flowering almond groves. He and Madame Paderewska loved attending movies, especially westerns and Charlie Chaplin films, accompanied by their dog, Ping, whom they smuggled into the theater hidden under a blanket.

When Paderewski returned to Riond-Bosson, he was refreshed and ready for hours of practice. He sacrificed his

Paderewski and Helena (in her official White Cross uniform) and
friends gather on the terrace of Riond-Bosson.

favorite game of bridge so scales, finger exercises, and pedaling could once again became part of his daily routine.
Throughout his life, Paderewski had gained praise for giving the piano "a new power" with his famous pedaling,
allowing even listeners in the far corners of the concert hall
to hear the tones he produced.

A well-prepared, but very nervous Paderewski returned
to the concert stage November 22, 1922, at Carnegie Hall:
Thirty-one years had passed since his debut there. His fears
were unfounded. The thundering applause demanded
encore after encore. One critic wrote, "five years in the purgatory of earthly experience have given Paderewski's art
fresh power, new significance."

During this first return tour, the sixty-two-year-old
Paderewski traveled eighteen thousand miles in his private

Paderewski often played to raise money for charities.

railroad car, played in twenty-three cities, and grossed almost half a million dollars!

Paderewski's new wealth gave him the freedom to continue the generosity that had always been his trademark. He performed benefit concerts and donated the money to hospitals and disabled veterans in America, France, Great Britain, Belgium, Italy, and Switzerland, trying to repay them for their aid to Poland during the war. Paderewski paid for monuments in Poland to honor president Woodrow Wilson and Colonel Edward Mandell House, Americans who had helped save Poland. And, in 1933 he gave concerts for unemployed musicians in England and the United States. If he heard of someone who was destitute and ill, he paid for their treatment. When he left a hotel, he tipped the entire staff.

Many children gathered each July 31st, the feast of Paderewski's patron saint St. Ignatius, to celebrate with him.

He loved giving presents. Paderewski sent grapes the size of plums grown at Riond-Bosson to the Pope at the Vatican. And when custom officials asked for some shoots from Paderewski's orchards to use to grow their own fruit, Paderewski generously accommodated them. They received more than shoots! He gave them whole trees wrapped in straw, tissue paper, and cord.

Paderewski's generosity was often reciprocated. Individuals and nations paid tribute to him. When a Paris audience discovered Paderewski's presence at a movie theater, the lights went on, and the audience rose to its feet. In French the words, "Long Live Paderewski. Long live Poland." filled the theater. Admirers hoisted Paderewski upon their shoulders and carried him outside to more cheering crowds.

The king and queen of Belgium rose from their seats to greet Paderewski as he appeared on-stage before a concert. Universities gave him honorary doctorates and his home at Riond-Bosson was filled with priceless treasures given as tokens of affection from admirers all over the world. He was decorated with the Grand Cross of the British Empire, and King George of England said he thought Paderewski was one of the greatest men he had ever met. "And the marvel of it all," stated his friend Colonel House, "is that the man remains unspoiled."

Amid the happiness of the years after World War I, Paderewski experienced a personal tragedy. Madame Paderewska, who began losing her memory, withdrew from the world. At times she didn't seem even to recognize him. For thirty years they had traveled together. He had often called her an angel and was often heard saying, "...there is no one like her in the world." When he had to go on tour without her, he arranged for the best of care. When he was home, he spent countless hours with her, holding her hand until she fell asleep.

He also worried about Poland, which still faced internal troubles and a serious threat from the Germans. His premonition that more trouble lay in store for Poland became stronger.

Paderewski also had his own share of medical problems. After recovering from a ruptured appendix operation and phlebitis, he prepared for another tour. During the fall of 1930 at age seventy, he began a triumphant eight month tour of eighty-seven concerts in the United States. A high point of the trip was a White House invitation from his good friend, President Herbert Hoover.

The following year in England, he had delivered up to eleven encores and autographed stacks of pictures. Flowers

Paderewski and musicians in Switzerland in 1926. Ernest Schelling, on the left, was Paderewski's pupil and conductor of New York Philharmonic Young People's Concerts (1924-29).

packed his dressing room. Grandparents took their grand-children to hear him so a new generation could experience his genius.

In 1930, at a banquet held in his honor in New York, Paderewski delivered a brilliant speech broadcast across the entire country. Since television had not yet been invented, millions listened to their radios as Paderewski presented the complex problem of Polish-German relations and Poland's need for an outlet to the Baltic Sea. He reminded his attentive audience that Poland's position and rights were being threatened.

On January 16, 1934, Madame Paderewska died with Paderewski at her side. She was buried at the Montmorency cemetery near Alfred, Paderewski's son. Paderewski was often seen at their graves gently arranging roses, flowers he had always avoided for fear the thorns might injure his fingers.

For two years after his wife's death, Paderewski refused public appearances although he spent long hours at home playing the piano. But in June of 1936 he agreed to star in the film *Moonlight Sonata*. Ads promoting the film read, "See and hear the world's greatest pianist." Critics didn't rave over the script, but fans who were treated to many close-ups of his hands traveling over the keyboard rejoiced that his piano playing is immortalized on the screen.

In February 1939, a weakened, tired Paderewski planned another American concert tour. Once again, he had given most of his new fortune away. This twentieth concert tour was a success, but it took its toll on his already failing health. On May 25, 1939, an audience of fifteen thousand waited for Paderewski's performance at Madison Square Garden. They were informed that the seventy-eight-year-old Paderewski had suffered a heart attack and their money

Lunch at Riond-Bosson: Paderewski's godchild Anetka watches as Macius, her black cocker spaniel gets a special treat from Paderewski.

would be refunded the following day. Members of the grief-stricken audience wouldn't accept their money back, but instead suggested that their refunds be given to Paderewski as "a token of the affection and esteem of his admirers." Five days later, Paderewski sailed for Europe.

A summer at Riond-Bosson, excellent medical care, and hours at the piano helped Paderewski's recovery. He needed his strength now: His premonition of trouble for Poland came true.

On September 1, 1939, Germany attacked Poland. World War II began. Warsaw and other Polish cities were being leveled by bombs. German orders for Warsaw were to shoot down everything standing and moving. Tragic news bulletins interrupted radio programming. As streams of displaced Poles filled the roads, they were bombed and machine-gunned from the air. Within the walls of Riond-Bosson Paderewski wept, played solitaire, and stayed near photographs of his late wife and son, contemplating how he could help Poland once more.

Chapter Nine

World War II

Soon after the outbreak of the second World War, the Russians attacked Poland from the east. Once again, Germany and Russia divided Poland. Many of Paderewski's countrymen, leaving everything behind, narrowly escaped to Romania before soldiers sealed the borders. Some Polish leaders who escaped to France established a government-in-exile to keep the Polish spirit alive. General Wladyslaw Sikorski and Wladyslaw Raczkiewicz headed this government, and they invited Paderewski to become the president of the National Council.

Professors, diplomats, and government officials flocked to Riond-Bosson to discuss Poland's situation, organize relief work, and gain advice on how to contact people who remained trapped in war-torn Poland. It seemed everybody in Poland knew Paderewski's Riond-Bosson address. Hundreds of desperate individuals begged him to trace missing relatives and deliver messages. His staff and friends assisted him in these overwhelming tasks.

In his study at Riond-Bosson, Paderewski prepared statements concerning Poland's troubles. He reminded the press that Poland's early resistance against Hitler had given the Allies time to prepare. As in World War I, he believed the Allies with America on their side, would come to Poland's rescue.

Paderewski also composed many letters and telegrams to prominent world leaders. Paderewski predicted Hitler would lose the war, and he warned Italy's Benito Mussolini that Italy shouldn't ally herself with Hitler. He implored Gandhi, the nonviolent leader of India, to give his moral support to Poland in her battle against Germany. Gandhi did and regretted that he was unable to do more. Gandhi wrote to Paderewski: "All that I can therefore send to the brave Poles is my heartfelt prayer for the early termination of their fearful trial."

In the spring of 1940, Hitler's army invaded Denmark, Norway, Holland, and Belgium. In the summer of 1940, less than a year after World War II began, the Nazi armies invaded France. France's tragic surrender on June 22, 1940, forced the Polish government-in-exile to flee to England. Where would Hitler attack next? Paderewski feared being cut off from the rest of the world. He must get to America where he could help Poland most.

With the Germans so close in France, Paderewski insisted that his sister Antonina, his valet Franciszek, and his secretary Sylwin Strakacz, Sylwin's wife, Aniela, and their daughter, Anetka, flee with him. Using the Cadillac that Herbert Hoover gave to Paderewski in Warsaw after the first World War as one of their vehicles of escape, Paderewski and his party embarked on the dangerous trip on September 23, 1940. As they left Switzerland and traveled through France, Spain, and Portugal, they were under Nazi surveillance. Even though French and Spanish border guards gave their protection to Paderewski and his group, trouble awaited them in Saragossa, Spain, where Spanish police placed them under house arrest for four days. It took

Paderewski and First Lady Eleanor Roosevelt, two humanitarians enjoy a chat in Palm Beach, Florida.

a telegraph from President Roosevelt to Spain's General Franco to get Paderewski and his group released. They finally reached Portugal, and in late October sailed for America on the small *Excambion* in the Nazi submarine-filled waters of the Atlantic.

Paderewski arrived safely in New York on his eightieth birthday to a great welcome. Crowds lined the streets, and hundreds of school children waved Polish and American flags. Paderewski felt honored that President Franklin Roosevelt sent his personal representative to greet him. Once again he was in America to make them aware of the tragedy in Europe. Human beings had been robbed, driven out of their homes or deported to die in concentration camps. He told reporters, "When more than one hundred million people are suffering. . . I simply could not remain an indifferent bystander."

As Paderewski made numerous appeals for his country, he appeared thinner and weaker. Worried that the Northeast winter would be too much for him, his physician ordered rest in Florida. Paso Robles was Paderewski's warm weather choice, but a California trip was too long and too expensive.

In Palm Beach, Florida, Paderewski rested, enjoyed the fresh orange juice from the groves, and shared a tender moment with a baby alligator that had been presented to his godchild, Anetka. One day, Anetka let the creature loose on the dining room table as Paderewski drummed his fingers on the table top. Onlookers worried that the alligator would bite Paderewski's hand. Paderewski remained calm and kept his fingers still. The alligator moved toward Paderewski and stroked Paderewski's fingers with its webbed foot. Then the baby gator nuzzled its head against Paderewski's hand and rested.

General Sikorski spent Easter with Paderewski in Florida to discuss ways of gaining more support from America, which still remained neutral. After enjoying a traditional feast of ham, eggs, and paska bread, Sikorski reported to Paderewski on the Polish government in exile.

Later that evening on an NBC radio broadcast, Paderewski reminded his coast-to-coast listeners that Poland was "the first nation, the first state to resist the Nazi aggression by force of arms." He denounced "the lies of German propaganda," which tried to lead the world to believe that the invaded countries approved of Germany's rule over them or at least were resigned to accept it. And in a hoarse, weak voice, he begged that democracy be preserved in Europe.

A few weeks after Easter, Paderewski was back in New York where he felt more at home. Even though he lost his appetite and his clothes hung loosely, he still worked hard for freedom.

Americans who tuned into their radios heard his request that they buy defense bonds to protect America's freedom. "I consider it a great privilege and honor to be asked by the Treasury Department to speak to you about United States Savings bonds." He expressed hope and confidence that Great Britain would defeat Hitler. "Stop Hitler before he masters the Atlantic," he pleaded. With Hitler defeated, there was hope for Poland and the world.

But the Allied victory was years away. On June 22, 1941, Germany attacked the Soviet Union. These two countries, once partners, were now enemies.

The next day at Oak Ridge, New Jersey, a weak and tired Paderewski spoke at a Polish war veteran's rally marking the twentieth anniversary of its founding. In the broiling sun he told a crowd of ten thousand that the future of the world was at stake. Aniela Strakacz remembered, "I thought the crowd would crush his car. Women with small children in their arms tried to force their way through the throng to get as close as possible to the president. People kissed his hands. Those who couldn't get that close tried at least to touch a piece of his sleeve or clothing and kiss that." It was Paderewski's last public appearance.

Paderewski battled with pneumonia for a week. He died at 10:59 p.m. June 29, 1941, five months shy of his eighty-first birthday, still believing that Poland would soon be free. One strong voice of freedom, the voice of small nations and oppressed peoples everywhere, was silenced forever.

People all over the world mourned his death. Flowers and telegrams poured in. The *New York Times* praised Paderewski's memory: "The warmth and generosity of his nature flowed not only into his music but into every act of his life." Following an ancient tradition often observed when great men died, Paderewski's heart was removed and carefully preserved.

President Roosevelt honored Paderewski by offering him a temporary resting place above ground at Arlington Cemetery until Poland was again free. (The law prohibits permanent burial in Arlington of any but native Americans who have served in the armed forces of the country.)

On July 3, 1941, Paderewksi's funeral mass was broadcast worldwide by shortwave radio. More than forty-five hundred mourners, including his sister, Antonina, who had played duets with him as a child, packed St. Patrick's Cathedral in New York City. Polish soldiers, dressed in the gray-blue uniform Paderewski loved, stood by Paderewski's casket draped with the Polish flag forbidden in Poland. In his eulogy, Archbishop Francis J. Spellman spoke of Paderewski's goodness and his dream of freedom for not only Poland, but for the world. The sorrowful, but hopeful, strains of Chopin's "Funeral March" filled the air.

Over thirty-five thousand men, women, and children, many of them with tear-stained faces, paid tribute as a funeral cortege of nearly five thousand proceeded down Fifth Avenue. A caisson drawn by six horses bore the body of Paderewski from St. Patrick's to Pennsylvania Station. A railway car that Paderewski had happily traveled in during his last American concert tour now transported his coffin to Washington, DC. As Paderewski's body lay in state at the Polish Embassy, the Italian ambassador came to lay a wreath in behalf of Mussolini.

Thousands lined the rainy path to Arlington, honoring this man who had dedicated his lifetime to freedom. Soldiers from the United States and Polish soldiers dressed in Canadian uniforms formed an honor guard. On July 5, 1941, at his burial, the United States army gave a nineteen gun salute, the highest anyone other than a chief of state can receive. His body was entombed above ground at the Memorial of the Battleship Maine at Arlington Cemetery awaiting burial in a free Poland. After the service, people recalled Paderewski's accomplishments. Who would become Poland's strong voice of freedom now?

Chapter Ten

The Long Journey Home

Fifty-one years after his first funeral, it was finally time for Paderewski to come home. Poland had found freedom.

On June 26, 1992, Paderewski's remains were taken from the Memorial of the Battleship Maine at Arlington Cemetery to begin its journey back to a free Poland. Thousands of Americans gathered at a public viewing at the Fort Myers Chapel, behind Arlington. The Polish flag, once again allowed to fly freely in Poland, covered the coffin.

The next day, Vice President Dan Quayle delivered the eulogy at a memorial service. "Today we send home a champion of liberty, a dreamer who made his dreams come true, an artist whose highest creation was his life of faith. This son of Poland, this citizen of the world, returns at last to a homeland free and independent...We celebrate, first the genius and the vision of a man whose music is as immortal as his soul. We celebrate, as well, the triumph of his people, the rebirth of their nation. And we remember, from his example, that, over the long run, history is shaped more by faith than by power . . . Paderewski's Poland has taught the world to sing again the songs of freedom."

The flag-draped casket was again set upon a horse-drawn caisson. The American government gave full state honors with the largest and most elaborate state funeral since President John F. Kennedy's.

At a dedication at Arlington on May 9, 1963, honoring Paderewski's memory, President John F. Kennedy stated: "It is no accident that men of genius in music, like Paderewski or Chopin, should also have been great patriots. You have to be a free man to be a great artist."

Paderewski's remains left the United States by plane for Poland and arrived in Warsaw on June 29, 1992, the fifty-first anniversary of Paderewski's death. As the motorcade made its fifteen-mile journey from the airport to Old Town Square in Warsaw, thousands of Poles, many who had endured years of suffering, openly wept and threw flowers, welcoming the remains of the man who had dedicated his entire life to guaranteeing Poland's freedom.

After several days of tributes, memorial services, and concerts, attended by tens of thousands of Poles, the funeral was conducted on July 5, 1992, at St. John's Cathedral in Warsaw, Poland. President and Mrs. Bush headed a U.S. delegation. Poland's President Lech Walesa, the man who in recent years helped bring democracy to Poland, attended. Paderewski's remains were placed in a crypt in the cathedral.

Later, President Bush spoke to over one million people who gathered in the Old Town Square on this historic occasion. "Today, a patriot has come home. Today, Poland is free. And what a magnificent day this is. On this Sunday, from St. John's Cathedral to the village churches of Zakopane, the bells toll not simply this solemn requiem, but a new beginning, a new birth of freedom, for Poland and its people."

Paderewski's heart remains in the United States, his "second country," at the Shrine of Our Lady of Czestochowa in Doylestown, Pennsylvania. Many journey each year to pay tribute to Paderewski's memory the way he once paid tribute to the noble hearts of his heroes.

The memory of Ignacy Jan Paderewski lives on—even though his fame has faded. His memory lives on as music students proudly play his *Minuet*, as school children in Paso Robles recite lines from a play in his honor at the

July 5, 1992 President and Mrs. Bush attend Paderewski's second funeral at Saint John's Cathedral in Warsaw. To the left of President Bush is Lech Walesa, then Poland's President.

Paderewski Festival, as a tree planted in his honor in 1941 still shades New York City's Tompkins Square Park, as Poles enjoy the freedom he never stopped fighting for, and as others try to emulate the sacrifices he willingly made his whole life through.

Pronunciation Guide

Polish is a rich and challenging language to learn. Phonetic transcription is imperfect, but the following pronunciation related to familiar English sounds of selected Polish words used throughout the text may be useful to the reader:

Biernacki (beer-not-skee)
Chodkiewicz (hod-kev-ich)
Chopin (sho pan)
Cielewicz (chee-lev-ich)
Czestochowa (chen-sto-ho-va)
Gdansk (gud-ainsk)
Ignacy (ig-not-see)
Jan (yawn)
Kosciuszko (Kosh-chu-shko)
Kurylowka (koor-il-ovka)
Lwow (luh voof)
Mickiewicz (Mits-ke-vich)
Modjeska (Modj ev ska)

Paderewski (pa-de-rev-skee)
Pilsudski (pill sood skee)
Poznan (poz-nan)
Sejm (same)
Sienkiewicz (shin-kiev-ich)
Sikorski (seek-or-skee)
Strakacz (stra kach)
Sudylkow (sood-il-kov)
Walesa (va-wen-sa)
Warsaw (var-saw)
Wilno (veel-no)
Zakopane (za-ko-pa-ne)
Zamek (za-mek)

For your information:
There is no letter v in Polish.
w is pronounced as v.
ow (a frequent combination in Polish) is pronounced as oof.
j is pronounced as y in you or boy.
There are no silent Polish letters, except "c" in "Ch"
pronounced as (kh).

Polish family names have special endings for women:
When the family name of the husband ends in ski, the name of the wife
would end in ska e.g. Madame Paderewska.

Timeline

1860	Ignacy Jan Paderewski born in Kurylowka, Poland (then a part of Czarist Russia).
1872	Begins formal musical studies at the Warsaw Conservatory.
1878	Graduates from the Conservatory.
1880	Marries Antonina Korsak. Son, Alfred born. Antonina dies.
1887	Debuts in Vienna, Austria.
1888	Paris Debut.
1890	London Debut.
1891	Begins first American tour.
1892-1893	Second American tour.
1894	Father, Jan Paderewski dies.
1896	Establishes the Paderewski Award to encourage talented American composers.
1897	Buys Riond-Bosson in Morges, Switzerland.
1899	Marries Helena Gorska.

1900	Son, Alfred dies.
1903	Spends a great part of the year composing, including Piano Sonata in E flat minor (op. 21) and Variations and Fugue in E flat minor (op. 23).
1904	Tours Australia and New Zeland.
1907	Composes Symphony in B minor, "Polonia" (op. 24).
1910	Delivers two important speeches in Poland.
1911	Tours South America.
1914	Purchases a ranch in Paso Robles, California; World War I begins.
1915-1918	Works on Poland's behalf in America. Meets with President Woodrow Wilson.
1918	Returns to Poland.
1919	Becomes Premier of Poland. Serves as chief delegate at the Paris Peace Conference and signs the Treaty of Versailles for Poland.
1920	Returns to Riond-Bosson; addresses the League of Nations.
1922	Returns to the concert stage at Carnegie Hall.
1930-1931	Conducts an eighth-month, eighty-seven concert tour of the United States.

1932	Delivers a speech in New York City titled "Poland and Peace."
1933	Gives benefit concerts to aid unemployed musicians in England and the United States.
1934	Madame Helena Paderewska dies.
1936	Stars in the film *Moonlight Sonata*.
1939	World War II begins.
1940	Serves as a leader of the Polish Government in exile.
1941	Speaks out against Adolf Hitler. Dies at the Hotel Buckingham, New York City. Temporarily entombed at Arlington National Cemetery until Poland is free.
1992	Paderewski's remains are finally returned to Poland for burial after fifty-one years.
1993	First Annual Paderewski Festival held in Paso Robles, California.

Nations Engaged in
World War I

CENTRAL POWERS

Austria-Hungary
Bulgaria
Germany
Ottoman Empire

ALLIES

Belgium
Brazil
British Empire
China
Costa Rica
Cuba
France
Greece
Guatemala
Haiti
Honduras
Italy
Japan
Libera
Montenegro
Nicaragua
Panama
Portugal
Romania
Russia
San Marino
Serbia
Siam
*United States

*The United States was the last major nation to enter the war, joining the Allies in 1917

Nations Engaged in
World War II

THE ALLIES

Argentina
Australia
Belgium
Bolivia
Brazil
Canada
Chile
China
Columbia
Costa Rica
Cuba
Czechoslovakia
Denmark
Dominican Republic
Ecuador
Egypt
El Salvador
Ethiopia
France
Great Britain
Greece
Guatemala
Uruguay
Honduras
India
Iran
Iraq
Lbebanon

Liberia
Luxembourg
Mexico
Mongolian People's Republic
Netherlands
New Zealand
Nicaragua
Norway
Panama
Paraguay
Peru
Poland
San Marino
Saudi Arabia
South Africa
Soviet Union
Syria
Turkey
United States
Uruguay
Venezuela
Yugoslavia

THE AXIS

Albania   Italy
Bulgaria   Japan
Finland   Romania
Germany   Thailand
Hungary

Program from Paderewski's First American Concert

Courtesy of James H. Phillips, Phoenix,
and Henry Z. Steinway, New York

MUSIC HALL,

First Concert, Tuesday Evening, Nov. 17th, 1891.

at 8:15 o'clock.

Paderewski's Inaugural Concerts,

——ASSISTED BY——

The Symphony Orchestra,

WALTER DAMROSCH, Conductor.

PROGRAMME:

1 OVERTURE, In Springtime . . . . . , *Goldmark*
ORCHESTRA.

2 CONCERTO, No. 4, in C minor, ... *Camille Saint-Saens*
Allegro moderato. Andante. Allegro vivace.
Andante. Allegro.
PADEREWSKI.

3 PIANO SOLI—*a*, Nocturne,
b, Prelude.
c, Valse,
d, Etude, . . . *Fred. Chopin*
e, Ballade,
f, Polonaise in A flat,
PADEREWSKI.

4 CONCERTO, No. 1, Op. 17, ... *Paderewski*
Alllegro. Romanza. Allegro molto vivace.
PADEREWSKI,

5 "RIDE OF THE VALKYRIES," . . . . . *Wagner*
ORCHESTRA.

Steinway & Sons' Pianos used at these Concerts.

The Second Concert will take place on
Thursday Eve'g, Nov. 19, at 8.15.

The Third Concert will take place on
Saturday Aft'n, Nov. 21, at 2:30.

Sources

CHAPTER 1
Boyhood Dreams

"What is happening to my father?" Paderewski, Ignace Jan and Mary Lawton. *The Paderewski Memoirs*, p. 5

"The French are safely at Cologne." Ibid., p. 24

"I did not lie. I only read what you had hoped - what you wanted." Ibid., p. 25

"a few hard whacks" Ibid., p. 25

CHAPTER 2
A Musical Life Begins

"You will never be a pianist. Never." Paderewski, op. cit., p. 42

CHAPTER 3
Striving for Musical Perfection

"I knew he would make a name and fortune. His poetic...." Phillips, Charles. *Paderewski: The Story of a Modern Immortal*, p. 102

"Poland needs you. Every man and woman of Polish blood must..." Ibid. p. 102

"You could have become a great pianist if...." Paderewski, op. cit. p. 83

"...so brilliant, like tiny, shining diamonds." Paderewski, op. cit. p. 90

"My experience was my armor..." Paderewski, op. cit. p. 156

"Paderewski, the Lion of Paris." Zamoyski, Adam. *Paderewski*, p. 42

"Much noise, little music" Ibid. p. 52

"Plainly we do not like Mr. Paderewski. The result of his...." Phillips, op. cit p. 131

"How nice it must be to look as fine as one is inside." Landau, Rom. *Ignace Paderewski: Musician and Statesman*, p. 35

CHAPTER 4
An American Welcome

"We hear you have had brilliant successes in London and Paris, but..." Paderewski, op. cit., pp.190-191

"seemed to speak a new language in music..." Phillips, op. cit., p. 172

"his fingers glide over the keyboard as if it were all done by electricity." Zamoyski, op. cit., p. 66

"...the actual physical strength required to produce a very big tone from a Steinway..."

Paderewski, op. cit., p. 220

"There is nothing I can do for you. You must rest." Paderewski, op. cit., p. 221

"I may never come this way again." Phillips, op. cit., p. 193

"struggling for recognition or encouragement" Phillips, op. cit., p. 223

"Our own initials were carved on the hidden parts of these stones, and..." Gilder, Rosamond, ed. *The Letters of Richard Watson Gilder*, p. 191

CHAPTER 5
"Paderewski and the World"

"I play only before audiences who listen to music and not their own talking." Paderewski, op. cit., p. 232

Madame Paderewska - In Polish even though her husband's last name ends in "i" the wife's last name takes the feminine ending and ends in "a"

"Look here have a drink - have a drink." Paderewski, op. cit., p. 355

"Who is there? Who is it?...."Oh, Lord, how beautiful." Paderewski, op. cit., p.356

"...something was happening to my nerves that made me completely..." Paderewski, op. cit., p. 366

"...The achievement upon which we look today was not born of hatred, but out of deep love..." Phillips, op, cit., p. 282

"...the nation cannot perish that has a soul so great, so immortal." Phillips, op. cit., 287

CHAPTER 6
World War I

"...lay between the territories of the belligerents who sought one another's throats" Buczynski, Theodore Joseph. *Ignace Jan Paderewski As An Orator,* (unpublished Master's thesis)

"It frequently happens that when the Red Cross go out to collect the wounded from a battlefield..." Phillips, op. cit., p. 306

"having stripped Poland of her robes, now offered her rags in return for the last drop of her blood." Zamoyski, op. cit., p. 155

"I take it for granted that statesman everywhere are agreed that there should be a united, independent, and autonomous Poland." "Text of the President's Address to the Senate" *New York Times*, January 23, 1917 p. 1

"countless numbers of Americans of the justice of the course Wilson was going to take."
Zamoyski, op. cit. p. 168

"free and secure access to the sea" McGinty, Brian "Paderewski" *American History Illustrated.* p. 69

CHAPTER 7
"Leading Poland"

"you must go there..go there and unite all the parties." Zamoyski, op. cit., p. 170

"If my husband felt any fear he did not show it." McMillan, Mary Lee, and Ruth Dorval Jones. *My Helenka*, p. 139.

"Suddenly a mumur rose from the crowd and grew to a crescendo of cries..." Strakacz, Aniela. From the Diary of; Translated by Halina Chybowska. *Paderewski As I Knew Him*, p. 5

"He seldom if ever spoke of it (music), but it was frequently noticed..." Phillips, op. cit., p.399

CHAPTER 8
"The Years Between Wars"

"For more than an hour Paderewski addressed this group in French..." Strakacz op. cit., p. 52

"The car with the Paderewskis in it inched along between a guard of honor consisting of two rows...." Strakacz op. cit., p. 68

"five years in the purgatory of earthly experience have given Paderewski's art..." Phillips, op. cit., 483-484

"And the marvel of it all is that the man remains unspoiled." House, Edward Mandel "Paderewski: The Paradox of Europe" *Harper's Monthly Magazine,* December 1925, p. 35

"...there is no one like her in the world." McMillan, op. cit., p. 188

"See and hear the world's greatest pianist" British Ad 1938 shown on the video cover of *Moonlight Sonata*

"a token of the affection and esteem of his admirers." Kellog, Charlotte. *Paderewski*, p. 200

CHAPTER 9
World War II

"All that I can therefore send to the brave Poles is my heartfelt prayer for the early termination of their fearful trial." Strakacz op. cit., pp.247-248

"...when more than one hundred million people are suffering...I simply could not remain an indifferent bystander." Mc Ginty, op. cit., p. 66

"the first nation, the first state to resist the Nazi aggression by force of arms." Strakacz, op. cit., p. 320

"the lies of German propaganda" Strakacz, op. cit., p. 320

"I consider it a great privilege and honor to be asked by the Treasury Department to speak..." *New York Times* "Radio Plea For Defense Bonds" May 17, 1941 p. 7 col 8

"Stop Hitler before he masters the Atlantic" *New York Times,* op. cit. p. 7

"I thought the crowd would crush his car. Women with small children in their arms tried to..." Strakacz op. cit., pp 327-328

"The warmth and generosity of his nature flowed not only into his music but into every act of his life." *New York Times* editorial July 1,1941 p. 22

CHAPTER 10
"The Long Journey Home"

(Quote under photo: "It is no accident that men of genius in music...."Public Papers of the United States, *Document 173*, p. 381-382

"Today we send home a champion of liberty, a dreamer who made his dreams come true, an artist..." "The Eulogy Given by Vice President Dan Quayle" *Sokol Polski: Polish Falcon,* August 1, 1992, p. 2

"Today, a patriot has come home. Today, Poland is free. And what a magnificent day ..." "President Bush's Speech in Poland" *Sokol Polski: Polish Falcon*, August 1, 1992, p. 4

Bibliography

Books

Baughan, Edward. *Ignaz Jan Paderewski.* New York: John Lane Company, 1908

Bruxner, Mervyn. *Mastering the Piano.* New York: St. Martin's Press, 1972.

Bukowczyk, John J. *And My Children Did Not Know Me. A History of the Polish Americans.* Bloomington: Indiana University Press. 1987.

Dubal, David. *Evenings with Horowitz: A Personal Portrait* New York: A Birch Lane Press Book, 1991.

Duleba, Wladyslaw, and Zofia Sokolowska. *Paderewski.* New York: The Kosciuszko   Foundation, 1979.

Finck, Henry T. *Paderewski and His Art.* New York: Whittingham and Atherton, 1895.

Gilder, Rosamond, ed. *Letters of Richard Watson Gilder.* Boston: Houghton Mifflin, 1916.

Hume, Ruth and Paul. *The Lion of Poland: The Story of Paderewski:* New York: Hawthorn Books. 1962.

Jedrzejewicz, Waclaw. *Pilsudski: A Life for Poland.* New York: Hippocrene Books, 1982.

Jones, Idwal. *Vines in the Sun.* New York: William and Morrow Company, 1949.

Kellog, Charlotte. *Paderewski. New York*: Viking, l956.

Landau, Rom. *Ignace Paderewski, Musician and Statesman.*
New York: Thomas Y. Crowell Company, l934.

Lansing, Robert. *The Big Four and Others of the Peace
Conference.* Boston: Houghton Mifflin Company, l921

Lengyel, Emil, *Ignace Paderewski Musician and Statesman.*
New York: Franklin Watts, Inc., l970.

McMillan, Mary Lee, and Ruth Dorval Jones. *My
Helenka.* Duraham: Moore Publishing Company, l972.

Mizwa, Stephen, ed. *Great Men and Women of Poland.*
New York: The Macmillan Company, l942.

Neuhaus, Heinrich. Translated by K.A. Leibovitch. *The Art of
Piano Playing.* New York: Praeger Publishers, l973.

Paderewski, Ignace Jan, and Mary Lawton. *The Paderewski
Memoirs.* New York: Scribner's, l938.

Phillips, Charles. *The Story of a Modern Immortal.* New
York: Macmillan, l934.

Pogonowski, Iwo Cyprian. *Poland A Historical Atlas.* New
York: Hippocrene Books, l988.

Reddaway, W.F. and J. Penson, O. Halecki, and R. Dyboski,
editors. *The Cambridge History of Poland.* Cambridge:
University Press, 1951.

Sandak, Cass R. *Poland.* New York: Franklin Watts, 1986.

Schickel, Richard. *The World of Carnegie Hall.* New York:
Julian Messner, 1960.

Strakacz, Aniela. From the Diary of; Translated by Halina
     Chybowska. *Paderewski as I Knew Him.* New
     Brunswick: Rutgers University Press, 1949.

Snyder, Louis. *The First Book of World War I.* New York:
     Franklin Watts, 1958.

Toor, Rachel. *The Polish Americans.* New York: Chelsea
     House Publishers, 1988.

Wandycz, Piotr. *A History of East Central Europe: The
     Lands of Partioned Poland 1795-1918.* Washington:
     University of Washington Press. 1974.

Walworth, Arthur, *Wilson and His Peacemakers: American
     Diplomacy at the Paris Peace Conference.* New York:
     W.W. Norton and Company, 1986.

Werstein, Irving, *The Many Faces of World War I.* New York:
     Messner, 1963.

Winter, Nevin. *Poland of Today and Yesterday.* Boston: L.C.
     Page and Company, 1913.

Wytrwal, Joseph A. *Poles in American History and Tradition.*
Detroit: Endurance Press. 1969.

Zamoyski, Adam. *Paderewski.* New York. Atheneum, 1982.

Articles

McCormick, Anne O'Hare. "Paderewski as the Symbol of a Tragic Era" *New York Times* July 5, 1941. p. 10, col. 5.

McGinty, Brian. "Paderewski." *American History Illustrated.* May-June 1991. pp.65-71

House, Edward M. Paderewski: " The Paradox of Europe." *Harper's Monthly Magazine.* December 1925. pp 30-36.

"America's Farewell to Ignacy Jan Paderewski," *Zgoda* July 15, 1992. pp 1-2

"American Tour 50th Anniversary," *New York Times* January 12, 1941.p. 29, col.1.

"Freedom's Symphony," *American Legion Magazine.* July 1991. p. 41.

"Homecoming For A Hero," *Time.* April 2, 1990. p. 25.

"Last Accord of Paderewski's Patriotic Symphony," *Zgoda* June 15, 1992. p.3.

"Paderewski Finally Returned to Poland," *Zgoda* August 1, 1992 pp. 2-3.

"Poland is Free. . .Paderewsiki is Home," *Polish Falcon* August 1, 1992. pp1-4.

"President Offers Arlington Grave," *New York Times* July 1, 1941 p.26, col. 4.

"President Wujcikowski To Attend Paderewski's Burial in
   Poland," *Polish Falcon* July 1, 1992 p.1

"Radio Plea for Defense Bonds," *New York Times* May 17,
   1941. p.7, col. 8.

Public Papers

Public Papers of the Presidents of the United States. *John F.
Kennedy Containing the Public Messages, Speeches, and
Statements of the President January 1 to November 22, 1963.*
Published by the office of the Federal Register National Archives
and Records Service. Document 173 pp. 381-382. U.S.
Government Printing Office Washington: 1964

Unpublished Master's Thesis

Buczynski, Theodore Joseph. *Ignace Jan Paderewski As A
   Orator,* (unpublished Master's thesis, DePaul University,
   1949)

Compact Disc Recording

Paderewski, Ignacy Jan. *The Art of Paderewski, Volume I* , GEMM CD 9499, Pearl Pavilion Records LTD, Sparrows Green, Wodhurst, E. Sussex, England.

(Paderewski's Chopin recordings are available on GEMM CD 9323 and Gemm CD 9397. Write to the above address for a catalogue and further information on the recordings listed here and more of Paderewski's work.)

Also check the internet
http://www.cdnow.com
http://www.steinway.com

Film

Moonlight Sonata. Starring Ignacy Jan Paderewski.
   Britain. 1938.

The Struggles for Poland. Once Upon a Time (1900-1923)
   Episode 1 PBS Video, 1988.

The Struggles for Poland. Occupation (1939-1945) Episode 4
   PBS Video, 1988.

Index

Acknowledgments

This book would not have come to be without the help of the following individuals and institutions. My deepest gratitude goes to them: Anne Strakacz-Appleton, Hy Blythe, James H. Phillips, and Christine Smith who encouraged me from the early stages of this project and offered excellent photographs and advice. I will never forget the kindness they extended to a stranger. Their deep devotion to Paderewski helps keep his memory alive; Remy Squires and Zbigniew L. Stanczyk of the Hoover Institution at Stanford University, Rita Rosenstiel of la Societe Paderewski in Morges, Switzerland, and Bronislawa Witkowska of the Naczelna Dyrekcja Archiwow Panstwowych in Warsaw, Poland for their kindness and additional assistance in obtaining photographs; Helen Dende who graciously translated correspondence from the National Archives in Warsaw, Poland; Kathy Abdalla, Dean Babcock, Linda Feller, John Sutkowsky, Carmella Todaro and staff members of the Scranton Public Library, Marywood University, and the University of Scranton who went out of their way to assist with research; Henry Z. Steinway, New York, Remigiusz Rudolf of the Museum of Ignacy J. Paderewski in Warsaw and Father Tim of Our Lady of Czestochowa Shrine in Doylestown, Pa, who were patient with my inquiries; The Kosciuszko Foundation, the Polish Arts and Cultural Foundation in San Francisco, the American Council for Polish Culture, the American Center of Polish Culture, the Polish American Cultural Network of Torrance, California, the Polish Falcons of America, the Polish National Alliance of North America, and the Polish Women's Alliance of America whose newspapers and newsletters crossed my path with articles that aimed to keep Paderewski's name in the news. (I know there are many other fine periodicals that celebrate Polish heritage that I haven't yet encountered, but hope to in the days ahead. I applaud them for their efforts.); Cindy Kane, Denise Lang, Marileta Robinson and Liz Rosenberg, my skillful mentors at writing conferences, who saw the manuscript at various stages and encouraged me to continue; John Riley, my publisher, who believed in this project; Susan Campbell Bartoletti, Lisa Rowe Fraustino, the late Norma DeNault Grula, Anna Grossnickle Hines, Mary Joyce Love, and Laura Lee Wren, members of my writers' group, who offered insightful critiques; the late Eleanor Wolfson and Wendy Wolfson who died on July 17, 1996, on TWA Flight #800, who both held Paderewski close to their hearts; Violet Rajchel Sharek (1892-1960), my grandmother, who was a great fan of Paderewski during her lifetime. Her devotion to him inspired me; My parents Leo and Gabriella (Sharek) Slivinski, my brother Dennis L. Slivinski, Father Andrew Bocianski, Father Joseph Brozena, and the Bernadine Sisters, especially Sister Charity who all taught me to explore and appreciate my Polish heritage and have respect for every culture; I am grateful to my friends and family for their love and support, especially my husband Carl, whose patience throughout this project has been remarkable.

Photo Credits

Illustration Credits

Archiwum Akt Nowych, Warsaw, Poland, Sygn 179/8, p.11, Sygn 214, p. 25; Courtesy of Anne Strakacz-Appleton, Rancho Murieta, California, pp. 67, 69, 71, 73, 77; Courtesy of Christine Smith, Rancho Santa Helena Collection, San Francisco, California, pp. 18, 23, 27, 31, 33, 35, 41, 43, 45, 51, 55, 68; George Bush Presidential Library and Museum, College Station, Texas. P33351-26A, p. 85; Hoover Institution Archives, Stanford University, Stanford, California, pp. 53, 59; Courtesy of Hy Blythe, Paso Robles, California, p. 65; Courtesy of James H. Phillips, Phoenix, Arizona and Henry Z. Steinway, New York, New York, p. 92; John F. Kennedy Library, Boston, Massachusetts, KN-C28377, p. 83; Courtesy of Societe Paderewski, Morges, Switzerland, p. 8.

Cover Photos

Courtesy of Christine Smith, Rancho Santa Helena Collection, San Francisco, California